IT'S A RED-EYED TREE FROG!

by Tessa Kenan

BUMBA BOOKS™

LERNER PUBLICATIONS ◆ MINNEAPOLIS

Note to Educators:

Throughout this book, you'll find critical thinking questions. These can be used to engage young readers in thinking critically about the topic and in using the text and photos to do so.

Lerner Publications Company
A division of Lerner Publishing Group, Inc.
241 First Avenue North
Minneapolis, MN 55401 USA

For reading levels and more information, look up this title at www.lernerbooks.com.

Library of Congress Cataloging-in-Publication Data

Names: Kenan, Tessa, author.
Title: It's a red-eyed tree frog! / by Tessa Kenan.
Other titles: It is a red-eyed tree frog!
Description: Minneapolis : Lerner Publications, [2017] | Series: Bumba books. Rain forest animals | Audience: Ages 4–8. | Audience: K to grade 3. | Includes bibliographical references and index.
Identifiers: LCCN 2016019519 (print) | LCCN 2016025863 (ebook) | ISBN 9781512425697 (lb : alk. paper) | ISBN 9781512429350 (pb : alk. paper) | ISBN 9781512427615 (eb pdf)
Subjects: LCSH: Red-eyed treefrog—Juvenile literature. | Rain forest animals—Juvenile literature.
Classification: LCC QL668.E24 K46 2017 (print) | LCC QL668.E24 (ebook) | DDC 597.8/78—dc23

LC record available at https://lccn.loc.gov/2016019519

Manufactured in the United States of America
1 – VP – 12/31/16

LERNER
e
SOURCE

Expand learning beyond the printed book. Download free, complementary educational resources for this book from our website, www.lerneresource.com.

Table of Contents

Red-Eyed Tree Frogs

Red-eyed tree frogs live

in rain forests.

These frogs live in trees.

Their feet stick to leaves

on the trees.

These frogs need a wet place to live.

Rain forests are very wet.

It rains almost every day.

Why do you think rain forests are good places for these frogs to live?

Red-eyed tree frogs are small.

Each one is smaller than a flower.

These frogs have big red eyes.

Red eyes scare animals that might

hurt the frogs.

Then the frogs can jump away.

Why do you think the red eyes scare other animals?

Red-eyed tree frogs have

green bodies.

Their feet are orange.

Their sides are yellow

and blue.

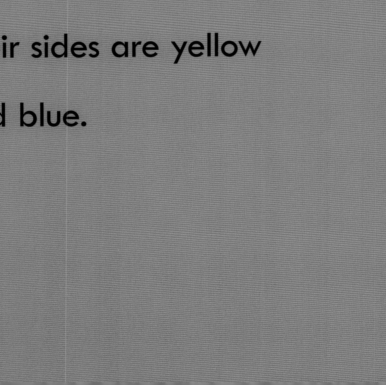

These frogs sleep during

the day.

They look for food

at night.

They catch insects

with their sticky tongues.

A mother frog lays eggs.

She lays them on a leaf

that hangs over a pond.

The eggs hatch.

The new tadpoles slide

down to the pond.

Why do you think the mother lays her eggs over a pond?

The tadpoles live in the water.

They grow legs as they grow up.

Then they climb out to live

in the trees.

Red-eyed tree frogs live alone.

They can live to be five years old.

Parts of a Red-Eyed Tree Frog

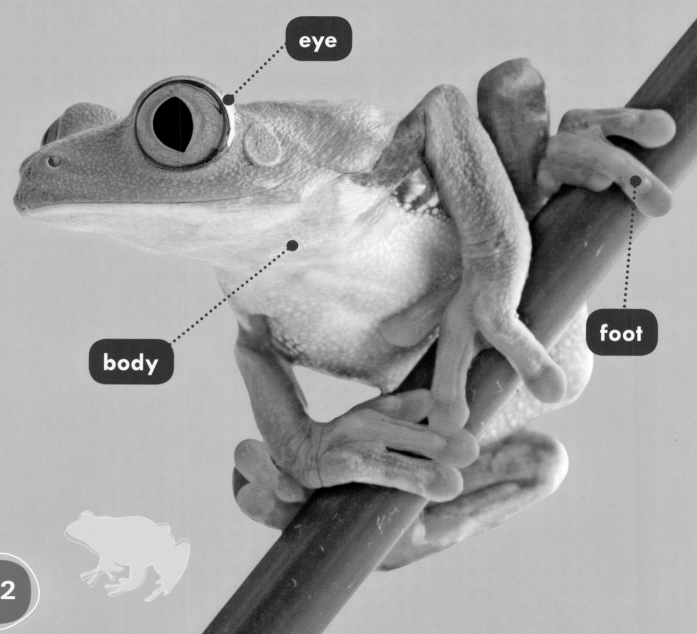

eye

body

foot

Picture Glossary

insects

small animals with wings, six legs, and three main body parts

pond

a small body of water

rain forests

thick, tropical forests where lots of rain falls

tadpoles

baby frogs

Index

Read More

Phillips, Dee. *Tree Frog.* New York: Bearport Publishing, 2014.

Raum, Elizabeth. *Poison Dart Frogs.* Mankato, MN: Amicus High Interest/ Amicus Ink, 2016.

Ringstad, Arnold. *Rain Forest Habitats.* Mankato, MN: Child's World, 2014.

Photo Credits